HOW TO DEVELOP AND LAUNCH
A DRINK BRAND

BY RICHARD HORWELL

DEDICATION

This book is dedicated to my Son Zavier
30/09/95-13/02/16, not a minute of a day goes by
that I don't think of you and miss you,
until that day we are together again.

I have been behind all of the brands within this book, whether it was creating the brand in its entirety or recipe development, brand name & messaging or product launch. There wasn't room for all 150 of them, so these are just some of my favourites.

- Richard Horwell

Hardcover ISBN 979-8-87079-947-6
Paperback ISBN 979-8-86703-763-5

Printed by Richard Horwell, in the United Kingdom.
First printing, 2022.

Branding Innovations Ltd

www.brandinginnovations.co.uk

TABLE OF CONTENTS

AUTHOR BIO

Richard Horwell has spent nearly all of his working life in FMCG, over 35 years living and working in the UK, USA, Australia and the Middle East. In 1999 he won Electrical Product of the Year for his 'VinChilla 4 Minute Wine Cooler', against many major players in the Industry. In 2012 he sold out of the company and moved to the US, then later to the Middle East. Missing the UK, he then returned to set up Brand Relations. Since this time he has been behind the launch of over 150 brands in food and drink, and most of these brands have been fully developed and branded by Brand Relations.

"The reason behind this book is to show anyone thinking about developing their own drink how incredibly hard this industry is. I see so many businessmen and their families invest everything they have into a brand and then it fails. This book will open your eyes to the challenges and pitfalls you may face, along with the shortcuts to help."

INTRODUCTION

Creativity has been booming worldwide since Covid. The pandemic shook the world up and changed people's attitude towards work. Many people previously employed in so-called 'safe' careers are not only deciding to move into a creative and a perceived recession-proof industry such as food and drink, but also wanting to be their own bosses.

Many budding entrepreneurs look at the range of drinks in the supermarkets or stores and say to themselves 'I can do better than that!', and they probably can, but starting a food or drink company isn't easy or cheap!

Many years ago, I went to a conference where they spoke about 'Ways to Fail'. The basic message was don't take money from a successful business and invest in something you know nothing about, as it's a sure way to fail. Hopefully this book will give you the best chance of success.

CHAPTER 1

Market Research

If you don't know where other brands have been, how will you know where yours is going? Look at their ideas and their mistakes, and learn from them.

THE COMPETITIVE ARENA

I can't state this strongly enough: Research your market! We have so many clients that come to us with very little idea of the competition in the category that they are planning to enter. The more established a category is— such as energy drinks, functional foods, luxury or free-from products —the harder and more expensive it will be to make any inroads.

Always check to see if your idea is already available in the market. Did you perhaps see it on holiday and think 'this is a good idea, let's do it here'? If it is a well-established brand overseas, the chances are they will have huge marketing budgets and be able to swallow any market you establish at home—so beware of that!

RESEARCH THE WORLD

Don't just look locally, research the rest of the world. You can learn a lot from other brands' mistakes and get some great ideas from the flavours they have used. Doing your research allows you to understand: others' messaging to their audience, how well they are selling in their market and at what retail price- all things that could inform your brand's decisions.

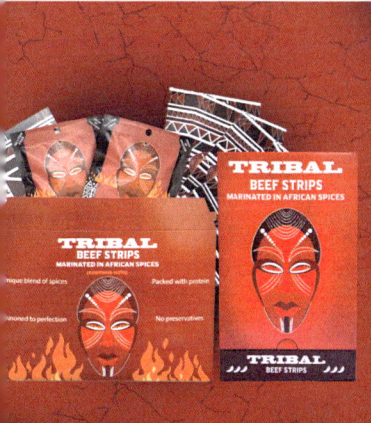

POINT OF DIFFERENCE

The key to doing well is having a product consumers will cross the road to buy. To do this you need to work out what your Point of Difference (POD) is so that you will stand out from the masses. This is crucial in order to have any chance of success in today's market.

Your POD needs to be very clear in your branding and messaging on the packaging. Just being vegan, for example, is not enough. Whilst vegan products were novel to the masses in the early 2010s, there is an abundance of vegan brands now, and when it comes to drinks specifically most of them are already vegan. Being organic isn't a huge head turner either. It makes production more expensive, and unless you're a juice then there's so few ingredients that it isn't worth it. Find out what's worth having to set you apart, marketing this is what will make you stand out.

So, sit down and think long and hard about what you are offering and why it will stand out in the marketplace. There has been A LOT of innovation in the F&B category over the last 10 years. Many small brands have become big brands and even taken on the likes of Coca Cola, so much so that the big players have spent millions to acquire them. This is the dream of any new brand but, in reality, it rarely happens and far too many products simply don't stand out anywhere near enough to make a real difference in the market.

On a practical level, think about what makes your brand different. Make a list of these points and then pick the MOST important ones. These are the ones you should highlight on the packaging. The less important ones still need to be on there, but they can go on areas the consumer will read once they pick the product up.

Whilst working on your list, keep in mind that to stand out from the crowd you must have a point of difference which means that your target audience will cross the road to buy your product rather than just accept what is on offer close by. Creating a following is what makes your brand attractive to the big players to buy in the long term; they want your audience.

Your point of difference is so much more than just a funky flavour or more eye-catching packaging. It means being truly unique—blending ingredients that others have not thought of before and most importantly making sure it tastes great!

ESTABLISH PROVENANCE

Customers want to understand the brand's heritage and values, who is behind the brand, what's their motivation? These are things that can set you apart. Today's consumers are becoming more and more socially conscious and want brands to be transparent. Is the product certified to be Vegan, Fairtrade or Organic? Which of these will resonate with your target audience? More recently, consumers are looking for certifications like 'B Corporation', which commends businesses that give as much consideration to their social and environmental impact as they do to their financial returns.

We worked with Can'O Water, a brand that has the reduction of plastic waste at its heart. They chose a simple, 'does what it says on the tin' name—after all it is water in a can, so why beat about the bush? They were ahead of their time in terms of playing to the consumer's new taste for ethical consumption and agile enough to adapt to the demands of their target consumer; they now even make their cans reusable with close caps.

This move towards wanting to buy from companies with matching values is an opportunity for new, indie brands because the established companies can't adapt as quickly. It takes time to remove artificial ingredients and replace them with natural ones, to change supply chains to Fairtrade/ethical sources or create a business that cares about the environment and its impact on our future. This is what today's consumers are looking for and this is what your branding should communicate in regards to your business. Made locally, can I support this brand for its beliefs and am I supporting my home market?

CHAPTER 1
take-outs

**Knowledge
is power**, you MUST
understand **as much**
as you can about
your market.

**You must have a
Point of Difference**
to what is already out there,
so consumers will cross the
road **to buy
your brand.**

**Values,
ethically speaking,**
what's **behind**
your product?

Recipe Development

There have been huge amounts of innovation in the food and beverage industry in the past 10 years, from flavours to functionality, consumers expect a lot more from a product now, it's up to you to 'wow' them with your ingenuity.

'INNOVATE DON'T IMITATE'

CONSUMERS BUY FOR HEALTH BUT RETURN FOR TASTE

Consumer buying habits are changing. When it comes to food and beverage, people are now much more focused on health and functionality. In the past, it was about buying into a lifestyle that a brand offered, rather than the actual product itself. In other words, brand loyalty was won by offering the consumer a sense of identity. Allowing a consumer to feel part of a community; the notion that you were 'cool' if you were to buy this product since only the 'richest' or 'best looking' would buy it.

With so many new brands and so much choice, consumers are now looking for products that will add value to their life, beyond simple hydration or filling a hole in a hungry tummy. If

you don't have a good reason for people to buy a drink, they'll stick to water, and tap water at that! So, when creating a new F&B brand, you need more than just aspirational promotion, you need to provide functionality and health benefits.

What do we class as a functional benefit? Functional snacks and beverages are those containing non-traditional ingredients like minerals, vitamins, amino acids, nootropics, fungi, dietary fibres, probiotics, added raw fruits, etc. All the drinks in the functional category aim to have some sort of effect on you other than just hydration. For example, Kombucha, Aloe Vera, Coconut Water, Green Tea and Moringa Tea are all examples of the new breed of functional drink flooding the market.

That said, while consumers might buy for the health benefits, they will only re-purchase and you will only build brand

loyalty if they love the taste! It's likely that flavour profiles were either part of your inspiration or part of your market research. However, just because you loved that flavour it does not mean you should simply seek to replicate it. You want something even better.

Be aware that old flavour favourites from childhood, like orange, blackcurrant or strawberry are very much giving way to more mature or exciting flavours such as rhubarb, elderflower, yuzu, etc. As you develop your flavour make sure it is ahead of the game and not lagging in the 'also-ran' section. Develop a brand for the future, not the past.

DOES IT TRANSLATE TO THE MASS MARKET?

So, you have the health benefits in hand and your flavour profiles sorted. Perhaps you have tried it on friends and family or sold it at the local farmer's market, but the hardest pill many of my clients have to swallow is the recipe will simply not taste the same when produced on a massive scale.

Your recipe at home has the option to be filled with the most expensive, best quality, freshest ingredients which provide the best end result. However if you want to mass produce a product then you may have to change ingredients to ensure the product isn't ridiculously expensive and can be mass produced cost effectively.

There are a few things to consider when contemplating the 'how' of mass production, shelf life (see next) and how are you going to mass produce your product.

Will you hire a commercial kitchen and bring in staff to help you make the product?

Or are you planning to take your recipe to an experienced manufacturer (co-packer) that will make and fill the product for you?

(For further details on mass production with a co-packer see chapter 4). A commercial kitchen will still only give you limited production and before you reach out to co-packers, you will need the help and guidance of a professional recipe developer, as what works in your home kitchen usually cannot be directly translated to mass production. These are things to carefully consider.

SHELF LIFE

The most important thing to consider is that your ingredients need to have a longer shelf life to adapt to the lead times of the route to market, whether this is via wholesalers and physical retailers or mail order. New products can spend far longer sitting on the shelf than established brands so you need to ensure you have that shelf life—this will save you money in the long run.

I knew of a lady who owned her own bakery which provided low-calorie alternatives to sugary cakes. It was a great product, but it only had 10 days' shelf life. This meant that by the time it ended up on the retailers' shelf it only had a few days left to be consumed— as a result, lots of stock went out of date and the brand failed.

Although generally the longer the shelf life the better, too long shelf-life products are viewed as unhealthy, so are less popular at the moment.

This is because often the only way to retain the shelf life is to put preservatives in your product.

In fact, many wholesalers and retailers refuse to accept products with high preservative levels as part of their range.

With this being said, try to look for alternatives, if at all possible. You can find the balance of keeping your product as healthy as possible, going through the wholessale system and onto the shelves long enough to sell. New products don't move very quickly.

Keep in mind you will need to adapt your recipe to ensure it will taste just as good at the end of its shelf life as it did at the beginning. As previously mentioned, professional recipe developers are the go to if you want to mass produce and this goes for shelf life as well. Food wastage is a big issue, financially and environmentally.

CHECK INGREDIENTS ARE LEGAL AND DESIRABLE

If your product is a novel food* check if the ingredients are legal. You can buy any ingredients online and add to a recipe for personal use but they may not be permitted on a mass scale for human consumption. Beware also of ingredients that may be legal in other countries but not necessarily where you plan to sell your product. Some products sold as supplements cannot actually be sold for mass consumption in food and drink. Check the regulatory agencies relevant to you.

For the UK, check the Novel Foods website: https://www.food.gov.uk/business-guidance/regulated-products/novel-foods-guidance

For the US, check the FDA's food ingredients and packaging: https://www.fda.gov/food/food-ingredients-packaging

And the FDA dietary supplements webpage: https://www.fda.gov/food/dietary-supplements

You need to look out for allergens such as milk or peanuts. If you are looking to work with a co-packer, many will refuse to fill your product due to the arduous process of informing each of their clients of the potential exposure.

Most importantly, you also need to make all allergens VERY clear to consumers and wherever possible remove them.

If not possible, ensure you find a co-packer that can cope with the allergens, and that your packaging makes them clear.

14 MAJOR FOOD ALLERGENS

CEREALS CONTAINING GLUTEN

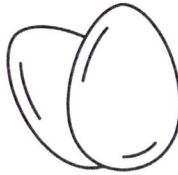

EGGS

FISH

MILK

TREE NUTS

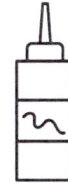

MUSTARD

CRUSTACEANS

PEANUT

SOYA

SESAME

SULPHUR DIOXIDE

LUPIN

CELERY

MOLLUSCS

CHAPTER 2
take-outs

Innovate,
don't imitate, create
recipes & flavours
for the future.

Consumers will buy for
health benefits
but return for **taste.**

Branding

Ninety per cent of a first sale is the branding. If you don't resonate with your target audience you could have the best tasting product on the market, but no one will pick it up off the shelf, so you will fail.

YOUR BRAND NAME

Surprisingly, the brand name is not the be-all and end-all, as it won't sell the product. BUT it is good to have something simple, and memorable in the long run, and / or a name that can communicate the product.

Start by researching your chosen brand name and make sure it is RELEVANT to your product and your audience. Be clever with your brand name, find something that is simple but conveys your product's message, not just a name that sounds fun to you and your friends and family. After all, some names can sound ridiculous—just because your friends say it sounds great, that does not mean it will resonate with your target audience.

We developed an award winning brand called 'Eternitea' which was a Collagen infused Tea available in Yuzu and Pomegranate flavour. Collagen is referred to within the beauty world as 'the fountain of youth' for it's incredible benefits in replenishing skin, hair and nails; so to play on it's functionality and the base of the product, tea, we got a memorable name that effectively communicated the product.

Once you have your name, or a shortlist, you need to check you can use it and you need to trademark it. With the growth in food and drinks products has come a rise in the amount of new brand names, which makes choosing the right name harder, and getting a trademark more challenging. Check your name hasn't been taken and can be trademarked.

For the UK check with:
https://www.gov.uk/topic/intellectual-property/trade-marks

For the US check with:
https://www.uspto.gov/trademarks/search

Whatever you choose, remember this name will be for the life of the brand, so make sure it has longevity.

MOST
INNOVATIVE
SOFT BEVERAGE

ETERNITEA

Gulfood
INNOVATION
AWARDS
— 2019 —

ETERNITEA
(COLLAGEN DRINK)

REFER TO MARKET RESEARCH

From your brand name, you can then work on the rest of your branding, by going back to the very beginning—your market research. Revisit this and ask yourself the following questions:

1/ **From the perspective of the consumer: WHAT'S IN IT FOR ME? This is the most important question, as that is all the consumer really cares about!**

2/ **What is my brand message? For example, is it based on health, functionality, treating yourself or great taste?**

3/ **Will my consumer be able to read the messages I have on the packaging from a distance, without picking it up?**

4/ **Does my brand look premium enough for the selling price?**

5/ **Why should a consumer buy my brand instead of their regular choice?**

6/ **What is the occasion in which the consumer will buy your product?**

7/ **Where will this product sell and what brands will sit alongside it? How will my product stand out against them? What products will buyers take off the shelves to fit your product?**

Getting the answers to these questions is the first step to creating brilliant branding. Today we have more choice of food and drinks than ever before and the big brands are no longer dominating the market. Many consumers want to try something different, but that doesn't mean they have all day to research every product. They need to be drawn to a brand that relates to them and says:z 'buy me, I am new and exciting'.

MOOD BOARDS

At this point, you can create a mood board. This is where you collate images, colourways, fonts and any other inspiration for your branding. Use the answers to your questions above to guide you and keep in mind what you are looking to achieve with every idea you 'pin' to the board. Be it physical or digital, it's important to keep in mind it's not just about creating an aesthetic you like, it needs to represent your brand and appeal to your target audience. Branding needs to show your customer why they should buy your brand, make it stand out on the shelf against any other brand existing on the market.

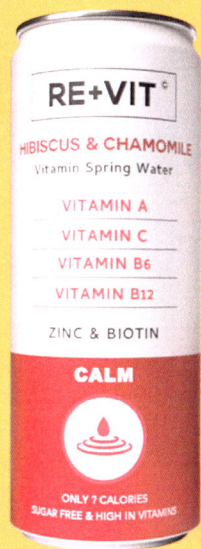

ESTABLISH MESSAGING: HOW YOUR PRODUCT WILL APPEAL TO YOUR TARGET MARKET

Make it easy for the consumer to choose your product fast.

Trade buyers only want products that will sell, they do not want old stock taking up room on their shelves. A product has to sell easily and quickly. Buyers won't give you long to prove that your brand works, it's in one day and out the next.

The key to establishing your message is ensuring it's easy to understand and includes elements that consumers can process instantly.

We all tend to pigeonhole everything in our lives and whether we are conscious of it or not, when we see a new brand, we automatically put it in a category. If you are attempting to break new ground with an idea or base ingredient then you need to add something to the mix that the consumer knows. For example, we recently developed a drink based on the Stinging Nettle and other garden botanicals. To encourage consumers to reach out and try this we have added ingredients and flavours they recognise, like gooseberry, cucumber and wild strawberry.

Minimalism has become a trend in recent years with many designs jumping on the bandwagon. However, be careful not to make it too minimal. I have seen some laughable branding where a designer has tried to be edgy but forgotten about telling the customer what's in it for them and actually selling the brand. This has led to the consumer ignoring it completely and reaching for the safer option; in other words, one of the established brands they already know. Find the right balance between doing too much or too little. You don't want to be too text heavy.

Let your branding do the talking.

A recent project of ours called Skinnytails, a range of low calorie cocktails, is a great example of using branding to show the customer what the product is and why it's appealing. In the UK—where these products are to be sold—you can't make health claims about alcohol, so the name and branding work together to show off that it's a low calorie and therefore most likely low sugar. Therefore appealing to customers who want a healthier alternative to the sugar filled premixed drinks on the market.

The most expensive word in this industry is "**education**".

EDUCATING YOUR CONSUMER

If you have to spend too long educating your consumer as to why they should buy your products then you will go broke doing so.

The best way to educate them is through the packaging. When they ask: 'what's in it for me?' and 'why should I buy it', these questions should already be answered when they look at the product on the shelf. Trade buyers and consumers need to understand the product without you standing there spelling it out. That's what branding is for; to provide instant understanding.

When I lived in Australia, I knew a very successful businessman who could turn his hand to anything. When I asked him his secret to success, his response was: "when you explain something to someone and they don't understand, it's not them who is being stupid, it's you who is not explaining properly". This is the same with branding. Just putting your brand name on the front and thinking the brand will sell is crazy. Consumers don't care about a 'new' brand name, they care about what's in it for them and I believe I may have mentioned that, but it's worth repeating as in the end it's what really matters.

CHAPTER 3
take-outs

The best way
to educate your consumer
is on the packaging.

It's all about the **consumer**,
you should be telling them
what's in it for them!

What's in a name?
it needs to be **memorable.**

Use your market **research**
to find out what you should be
saying, and who you're
saying it to.

Let your branding
do the talking
consumers should "get it"
without you spelling it out.

BALANCE
supplement

15 servings

glotone
confidence drink

INOSITOL
MAGNESIUM
ARTICHOKE
MACA
MORINGA
ZINC
PROBIOTICS

SKIN GLOW
supplement

15 servings

glotone
confidence drink

VOLAGEN
BAMBOO STEM
CO Q10
VITAMINS A,B5,C,E
SELENIUM
BIOTIN
PROBIOTICS

TRANQUILITY
supplement

15 servings

glotone
confidence drink

LEMON BALM
MAGNESIUM
L-THEANINE
RHODIOLA
GINSENG
CHAGA
VITAMIN B5
PROBIOTICS

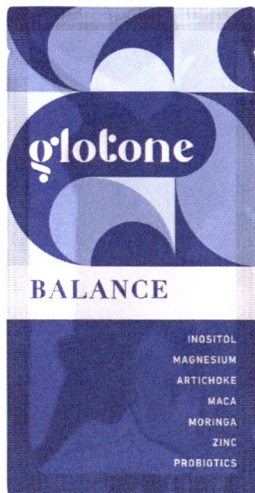

glotone

BALANCE

INOSITOL
MAGNESIUM
ARTICHOKE
MACA
MORINGA
ZINC
PROBIOTICS

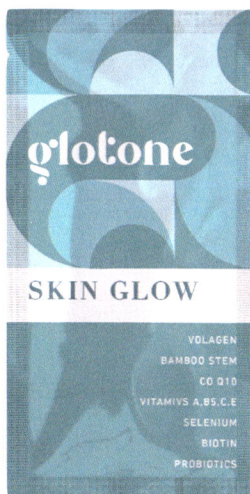

glotone

SKIN GLOW

VOLAGEN
BAMBOO STEM
CO Q10
VITAMIVS A,B5,C,E
SELENIUM
BIOTIN
PROBIOTICS

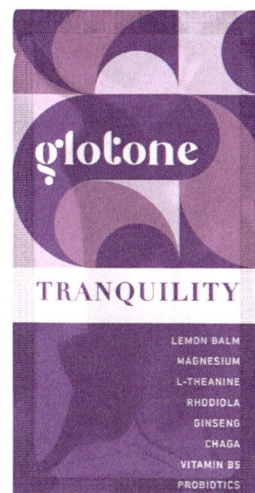

glotone

TRANQUILITY

LEMON BALM
MAGNESIUM
L-THEANINE
RHODIOLA
GINSENG
CHAGA
VITAMIN B5
PROBIOTICS

Packaging & Production

You've put in a lot of work already. Now to turn all that research, planning and fine tuning into an actual physical product.

SELECT THE RIGHT PACKAGING

There are many different options when it comes to packaging your product and choices you make can make a huge difference to your cost outlay.

Glass is the cheapest option as you can do the smallest production run. But, neither wholesalers or retailers like glass. The former due to the weight, and the latter because it may break—making it by far the hardest to sell. Also, if you are considering mail order, this is a bad idea for obvious reasons.

Hot Fill PET bottles are second cheapest in terms of small production runs, they can be filled with high temperatures in order to keep things sterile. The negatives are that the bottles are ugly with solid ridges down them and with the backlash of PET polluting the oceans consumers are turning away from this type of packaging.

Aseptic Fill is where the PET bottles are blown on-the-line and then filled in aseptic conditions to keep all the germs and so on out—after which the contents are pasteurised in the bottle, locking in all the nutrients.

However, you cannot do a small run with this method. The minimum runs are substantial as the factory needs to completely clean the entire line in between flavours—and with productions running at 25,000 per hour, you can imagine how many you'd need to produce to make this a viable option.

Cans is the next option. These are very popular now, but minimum runs are high. For example, minimum runs for printed cans are 150,000 and minimum filling runs are 75,000. There are options to fill blank cans from as low as 12,000 cans and then sleeve them afterwards. It is a more expensive option but a far better way to test the market.

Tetra Pak is fifth in terms of pricing, but the printed runs of the cardboard are around 100,000 per flavour and need to be used up within a year. **It's a risky option until you have the volume to justify it.**

Last, but not least, is **HPP**—High-Pressure Processing. This is great for juices as the temperature is only 4°C, so it preserves all the goodness, antioxidants and flavour.

The runs are small, but the cost is 10-15p per bottle just to put them in the machine since they use pressure instead of heat to pasteurise. The distribution must be chilled and has only a one or two-month shelf, which makes the product more expensive and adds risk.

Whichever packaging you choose, there may be the option to do a small run, but even so, you may find these initial production runs to be far more expensive than you'd think. Suppliers will often have minimum order requirements for the ingredients that are far greater than the amount you need for a small run. You will need to budget for this so beware.

Understanding the best type of packaging for your drink and your target market is important—it's a large part of your initial outlay so you want to get it right. A wrong decision could leave you with a lot of very expensive unusable product on your hands.

CO-PACKERS

In chapter 2 we spoke briefly about the "how" of mass-production. Here I'd like to delve a bit deeper into the option of Co-Packers. They are, essentially, contract manufacturers. These are the people that fill your drink in bulk. They are a hugely important part of the process, therefore you need to be careful who you choose to work with. Although there is a lot of choice in both the UK and EU, there will always be companies that care more about making money than they do about making the perfect product. Then, there are the big players that just don't care about start-ups. Whichever co-packer you decide to go with ALWAYS make sure they have the right certification, as once you start to get listings, this question will be asked by retailers and wholesalers.

Do your research and make sure that the company you select has a good reputation—maybe speak to other brands they have filled?

Also bear in mind that you are not calling all the shots. The relationship with a co-packer works both ways and they will be looking at volume. Unless you can give them confidence this project will grow and fast, then very few will consider taking it on. They also need to believe in your product as much as you do, so before you speak to them make sure your company and brand looks professional. Simple things should be considered: such as having an internet domain set up under your company name, so you are not emailing from a basic Gmail or Hotmail address. This will increase the likelihood that they take you seriously, so get brand ready.

COMPLIANCE CHECKS

As with anything, there are bureaucratic hoops to jump through to make sure things are legal and compliant. We've spoken about making sure your ingredients are legal, but you must also ensure the wording on your nutritional information and labelling is correct and complies with the law in the relevant country.

Barcodes put the GS1 link in. You will need barcodes for each flavour, and one for each case of these individual flavours.

All drinks attract VAT, check local regulations. Many snack and drink brands are VAT-able so you may need to be VAT registered.

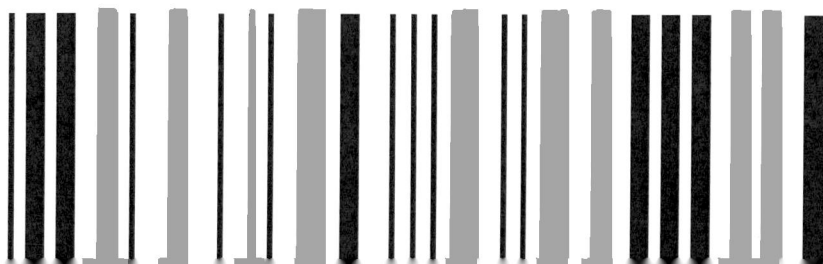

take-outs

Packaging that works for others may not work for you, choose wisely for your product.

Look for the right Co-Packer who **believes** in your product, and will work with you in the initial stages.

It's a two way street, **you need to** instil your co-packer with **confidence** too.

Marketing to Buyers

Selling to buyers is not simple, many of them won't even reply to your calls or emails. These days they are inundated with new products, so you need to persevere. Here are the steps to make that journey easier.

CREATE A STRONG MARKETING PLAN

Things don't always go to plan, but planning ahead and ensuring you have a timeline of when you will do everything leading up to approaching your buyer is crucial.

A lot of food and drinks sales depend on seasonality.

For example, the key time for soft drinks to sell is in the warmer months from Easter to September. This means soft drink buyers do their range reviews in January, February and March; this is so that new brands can hit the shelves after Easter ready for the Spring / Summer boom. Seasonality is mainly an issue if you are chasing the Majors. If you miss this time frame, it doesn't mean you can't sell your product, but you need to find out when your target buyers are doing range reviews. Premium retail and smaller outlets buy all year.

So, if you are aiming for success next summer, for example, January is the time when you should be presenting your product to the major buyers to ensure your brand is on the shelves for that season. You must stick to your plan. If you let it slip, you will find yourself so far behind you may have to wait another whole year until you can launch!

DRAW UP A LIST OF TARGET BUYERS AND RESEARCH YOUR TARGET RETAILERS

Before you decide which retailers you want to target, find out at least a little about them. And be sure you know what they are looking for. Just because you want to be listed by someone, doesn't mean you are right for them and vice versa. So do your research, a little preparation now will save you time and money later.

Try and look at the industry as a pyramid that you start at the top of and work your way down. Going in at the bottom or 'mainstream' and trying to go upwards simply doesn't work. Many brand owners come to me and say they want to be stocked in a large supermarket and my response is that they need to take what they can get. The best advice is to work with the relevant retailers that want to work with you and build your brand from there. The key word being relevant. I am not suggesting you take just anything that is thrown your way (in particular this applies to the big 'discounters'), but I am saying that if a buyer believes in your brand and they are smaller and fit more in the top of the pyramid, then try to explore and support that buyer in their stores and you can begin to build a reputation for yourself and your brand.

Many new brands want to go straight to the Multiples (large supermarket chains), looking for instant volume. But that is a mistake. You need to cut your teeth on the smaller 'premium' retailers and build the brand. I have seen a lot of brands go into one of the big retailers on a trial and then, after a few months, they have been delisted.

Once delisted by a larger retailer, none of the premium retailers are interested.

As you begin to understand where you are targeting, find out which buyers you will be contacting. As we've discussed, start small and then move big. Go and visit the stores and envisage where you would be sold, as buyers will ask you that. Keep in mind that customers in the likes of Whole Foods and Planet Organic are prepared to take the time to look for, and understand, new brands. Whereas the typical supermarket shopper is in there to grab the weekly shopping and get out.

The biggest issue in getting a listing with your target retailer is understanding their shoppers' needs. I have been told many times by buyers: "our fridges or walls don't stretch", meaning they need to remove a brand to put yours in.

How can they be sure your brand will replace the volume of the one they remove?

How will consumers know your brand?

Why will they cross the road to buy it?

All of these questions need to be answered before you have any chance of getting a listing.

I have a saying: 'no buyer wants to be first, but no buyer wants to be last'. If others see your brand selling, then you have a good chance of getting more listings elsewhere.

MARKETING FEES WITH WHOLESALERS AND RETAILERS

You need to be aware that there will be costs involved in getting your products onto the shelves. The main route to market for new brands is through wholesalers. They have established clients, know who the buyers are and what they want, as well as having systems to help stores re-order when stock is low. They can also raise and collect invoices.

The only issue with wholesalers in the UK and EU is GDPR: General Data Protection Regulation. GDPR is rampant in the UK and EU and means wholesalers can't tell you who their clients are. This can be a big hurdle to overcome, as you have to rely on their advertising or sometimes nonexistent sales force.

Selling direct to stores is almost impossible.

Many won't even deal directly as it's just too much aggravation to contract with lots of small independent suppliers. There's no central system for re-ordering when stock is low and lots of small invoices to pay—all of which is inconvenient and time-consuming.

Naturally, when you began your product development, you researched your target consumer and where they shop. This should have given you a list of target retailers. From there you can contact the relevant wholesalers and persuade them to give you a listing. Once you've sourced those wholesalers, as well as convincing them to give you a listing you must inevitably pay their listing/marketing fees. So be very aware that stocking at wholesalers isn't cheap. You may be asked to spend a minimum £2,000 listing fee per wholesaler, before your product is even advertised in their catalogues. This doesn't include the additional marketing which involves you providing the banners, e-flyers and any other materials for them. Some wholesalers demand the marketing budget to be paid in full upfront before they even place an order. Even then, the order is sale-or-return!

Many start-ups dream of being stocked by the larger supermarkets. Although this might seem like a great idea and a good alternative to the cost of stocking through wholesalers, it is generally not advisable, at least at first. Why? Because it is an almost sure-fire way to kill your brand quickly. Consumers shopping in supermarkets already know what they want before they've left the house; they do not have the time to learn about new products. And since the pandemic, they are even keener to be in and out as quickly as possible.

Frankly, supermarkets are ruthless, as are some of the larger chains.

For example, a UK based supermarket was charging approximately £170 per store, per product, just to list new products, without any kind of marketing from their point of view. This added up to a lot for brands wanting to be listed in lots of stores. They have stopped now, only after the press got hold of the story. However some big chains will still charge in the hundreds of thousands just to put your product on their shelves and I do not recommend paying that.

Despite rarely charging anymore, supermarkets will still do very little to promote your brand. It is likely to be put at the end of an aisle with lots of other new products, with no association to one another and absolutely no talking up of those new brands.

Despite all the cost considerations I have pointed out, it is still essential that you redirect as much business as you can to your chosen wholesalers and don't try to circumvent them. If they are making money selling your product, they will maintain the listing—and that's what you need.

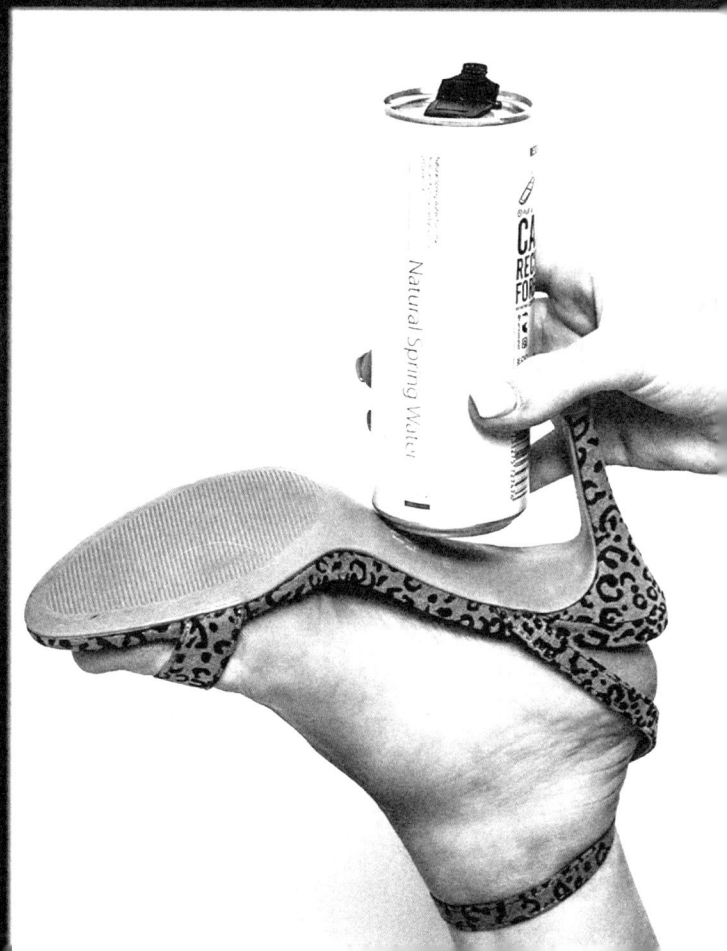

SAMPLE BOXES

Sample boxes are a great way of getting interest from buyers. If you have a great product, show them, better yet show them the product as a beautifully presented gift.

I have known many brands that have just sent a case of their product to a buyer hoping that somehow a lot of product will magically make the buyer interested. However, this is not a good approach. Buyers generally really dislike this, as most of them have small offices and the last thing they want is to fill them with hundreds of free products.

Do not send unrequested samples to buyers, as that does more harm than good to your brand.

A lot of brands also forget that buyers are consumers too. And just like any consumer, the first impression is the most important. We suggest our clients create sample boxes with a brochure to further explain the benefits and the marketing materials that you will have to support your product. These brochures should educate trade and where appropriate, demonstrate POS (point of sale) information that will encourage consumers to buy from the shelf.

The box should look great and have your branding and information on it. A few years ago, we put together some Christmas hampers made up of all the brands we were working with at the time. The response was incredible. One buyer rang and thanked us, but said he was sorry, as he wasn't allowed gifts. He was very surprised when we told him they were samples, as they were presented much more like a gift than a 'freebie'.

We believe in a healthy mind and a healthy body.

Our mineral water comes from the Mediterranean mountains.

ZERO SUGAR

ZERO CALORIES

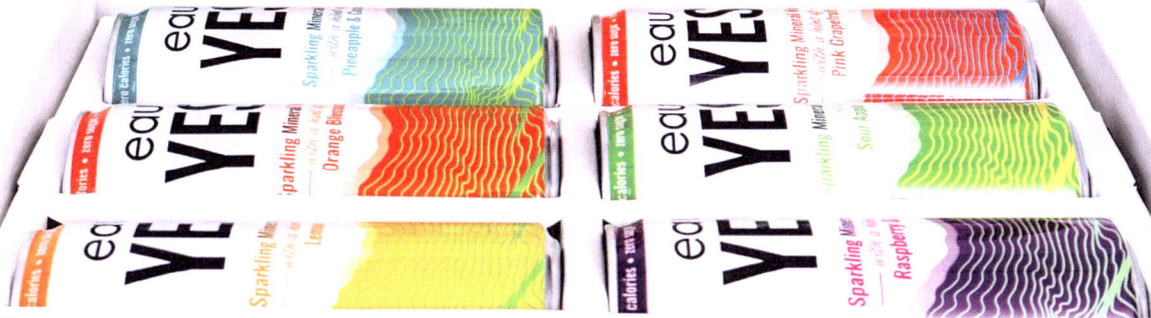

Pineapple & Coconut

Orange Blossom

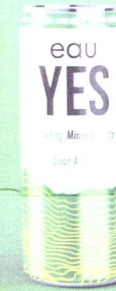

Raspberry & Lime

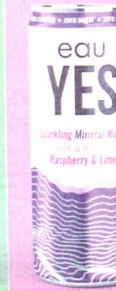

eau YES — Sparkling Mineral Water with a hint of Pineapple & Coconut

eau YES — Sparkling Mineral Water with a hint of Orange Blossom

eau YES — Sparkling Mineral Water Lemon

eau YES — Sparkling Mineral Water Pink Grapefruit

eau YES — Sparkling Mineral Water Sour Apple

eau YES — Sparkling Mineral Water Raspberry & Lime

f ⃝ ♪ @eauyeswater

ONLINE PROMOTION

Getting your website right is important—it is your shop window to the world! In your product's early days, it is used mainly as a showcase to trade buyers looking into your brand, but once you launch to consumers it will also need to be your online shop. It is an important tool that will help generate online sales and explain to customers why they should buy into your brand.

If necessary, get professional help, and be prepared to invest in your website, your advertising, your ecommerce system and your imagery—

after all everything sells better if the imagery is attractive.

It's essential that your website is easy-to-use and has a robust ecommerce system that includes: shopping baskets, accounts for returning customers, FAQs and detailed information about the product and brand story. Since the pandemic, many more consumers are likely to go direct to companies to buy their product.

Think about what questions consumers and buyers are likely to ask and ensure the website answers them before they have to ask- you'll only get one chance at this. Your website is your window to the World and what your product is, so make sure it looks enticing, informative & professional. It should be something to be proud of.

SEO is often considered the be-all and end-all. However, although I suggest perhaps spending a little to up your SEO on unique factors of your product, it is not worth spending money to compete with the big boys on terms like 'energy drink' or 'functional food', for example. What you have to invest will be a drop in the ocean.

Another route to your target consumer is to go direct. This is known as 'direct to consumer' or D2C. It involves utilising social media and third-party platforms which manage your sales for you, like Amazon, Shopify and Woo Commerce; plus online advertising to bridge the conversation directly between your brand and the consumer. Each platform will take a cut of the sales you make and some may charge a monthly fee as well. However, they are worth considering as they have their own customers already who trust the items they sell. So, it's a great way to reach people—but you still need to do your own marketing.

SOCIAL MEDIA

Just as importantly, you need activity on your Social Media. More recently the bigger stores have employed Social Media experts to look around for the brands that have the most interest and followers, then they contact them for more details. Why do they do this? Because your activity and followers give them a good indication of how well your brand will sell.

If your social media is looking a bit lacklustre start building it right now! Ask friends and family to follow your accounts and interact with your posts. Also start following relevant influencers, sales outlets where you want to be stocked, and, if possible, the buyers themselves. Start to create a buzz around your product and connect with people you'd like to work with.

Although social media is free in principle, be prepared to pump money into advertising on TikTok, Facebook or Instagram as that will help you gain traction and get your brand known; the more followers and conversations you have, the more attractive your product is to a buyer or investor. For example, one client we worked with sold all his stock on Facebook. It was a unique product which utilised the opportunity of COVID, when their target consumers had the time to educate themselves on the point of difference.

EXHIBITIONS

Exhibitions are something to consider as they can be a good way to present your product to buyers, but finding the most suitable ones, once again, requires research and planning. A stand at an exhibition starts from around £3,000 plus any additional costs. This may include travel, accommodation, stand dressing and promotional materials like banners, brochures, samples, etc. So it's something you want to think about before incurring those costs.

The people selling the exhibition space will make it sound so easy, but it's not. You need the right exhibition, with the right buyers, and a lot of hard work to generate worthwhile leads. Indeed, these days very few buyers take the time to visit the shows—they are simply too busy. Many of my buyer friends have told me that they have to go to exhibitions in their private time, as their Head Office no longer sees them as relevant. Whatever exhibition you choose, be very careful with what you spend and make sure it's a well-targeted and well-marketed show.

CHAPTER 5
take-outs

Plan your approach, know your target timings and **audience.**

Start form the top of the pyramid, **large retailers** aren't always right for you.

Sending samples isn't simple, do them **right** and **dont send** indiscriminately.

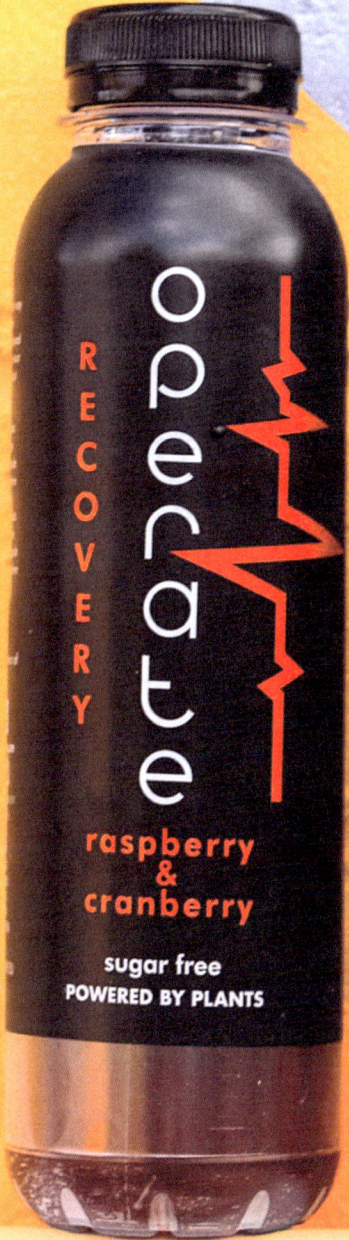

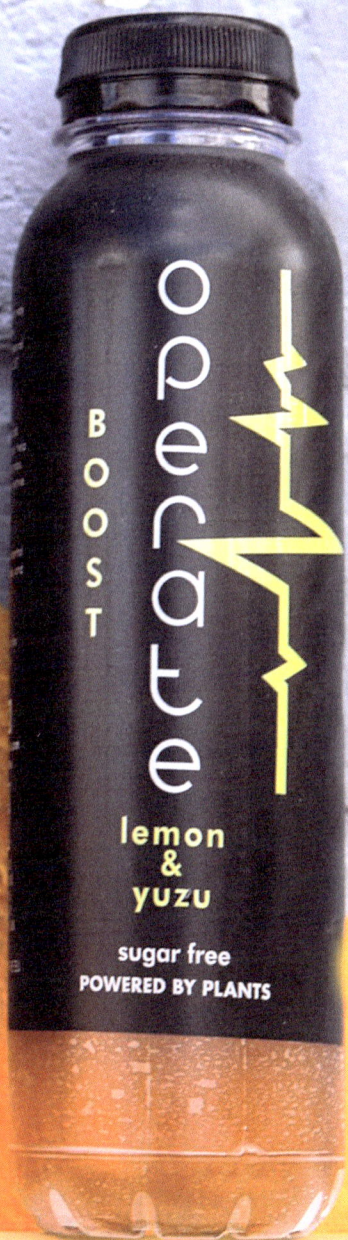

CHAPTER 6

Export

THE BENEFITS OF EXPORT

Exports can be the most lucrative part of selling your brand; International companies will buy the product and usually pay upfront.

This is a great option as they will do their own marketing, usually by their inhouse team and help towards making you a Worldwide success. However, I recommend that for all early orders they pay pro forma, as it's virtually impossible to chase debt overseas. With my own drink, Ibiza Ice, around 90% of our sales were International. This was achieved by displaying our products at exhibitions all over the World.

Exhibitions can be expensive but if you look into it you'll often find that Governments will support your endeavours in order to encourage export. In an ideal situation, you work on your home market as an example of how well the brand sells. This gives you a strategy to educate the importers as to how they can develop the brand locally to them. This isn't always how it will work, as in my experience sometimes the markets outside of your local one will be bigger and the strategy will be totally different.

The price you sell to them is usually lower than your price to local wholesalers, as there is no marketing spend required. However what I did was instead of giving any cash in support of the International marketing, I gave them an element of free stock only on the first order. Usually this encouraged them to order more since subsequent orders did not include free stock. Please be aware there can be a lot of liars and time wasters in International, so try not to invest too much time in this field

The best response was from a buyer at **Whole Foods**, who said;

"Thank you for sharing with us your innovation, highly appreciated, some other people I would expect this from are not doing half what you did! Thanks."

WHOLE FOODS MARKET

Needless to say, we got the listings we wanted with that buyer. So, put some time, effort and resources into creating sample boxes that will grab the buyers' attention.

FINAL WORD

The F&B industry is much like most new businesses; you will be lucky if one in ten will survive beyond two years. Make sure you are in that ten per cent.

Going from a fantastic idea, or perhaps a kitchen hobby to a genuine business is a huge step for any new start up. Selling weekends at farmers' markets or to friends and family unfortunately doesn't mean you are the next Levi Roots. It's a long, slow journey and can be a very expensive one if not done correctly. Think hard and research well before you do anything. Although the food and drink market is very tough and a lot of brands fail, it's also a fun industry and I wouldn't choose to do anything else.

My final word is to plan, plan, plan. As they say; if you fail to plan, you plan to fail!

This book is intended as a practical and no-nonsense aid for anyone who is looking to launch an F&B brand. I hope it will give you true insight into the industry and the journey you have ahead. I sincerely wish you and your brand the very best of luck!

Thank you and
I wish you
all the best

www.ingramcontent.com/pod-product-compliance
Lightning Source LLC
Chambersburg PA
CBRC090851210326
41597CB00008B/161